WOMEN

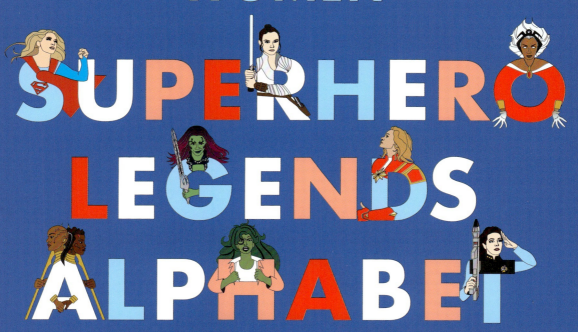

SUPERHERO LEGENDS ALPHABET

Words by Robin Feiner

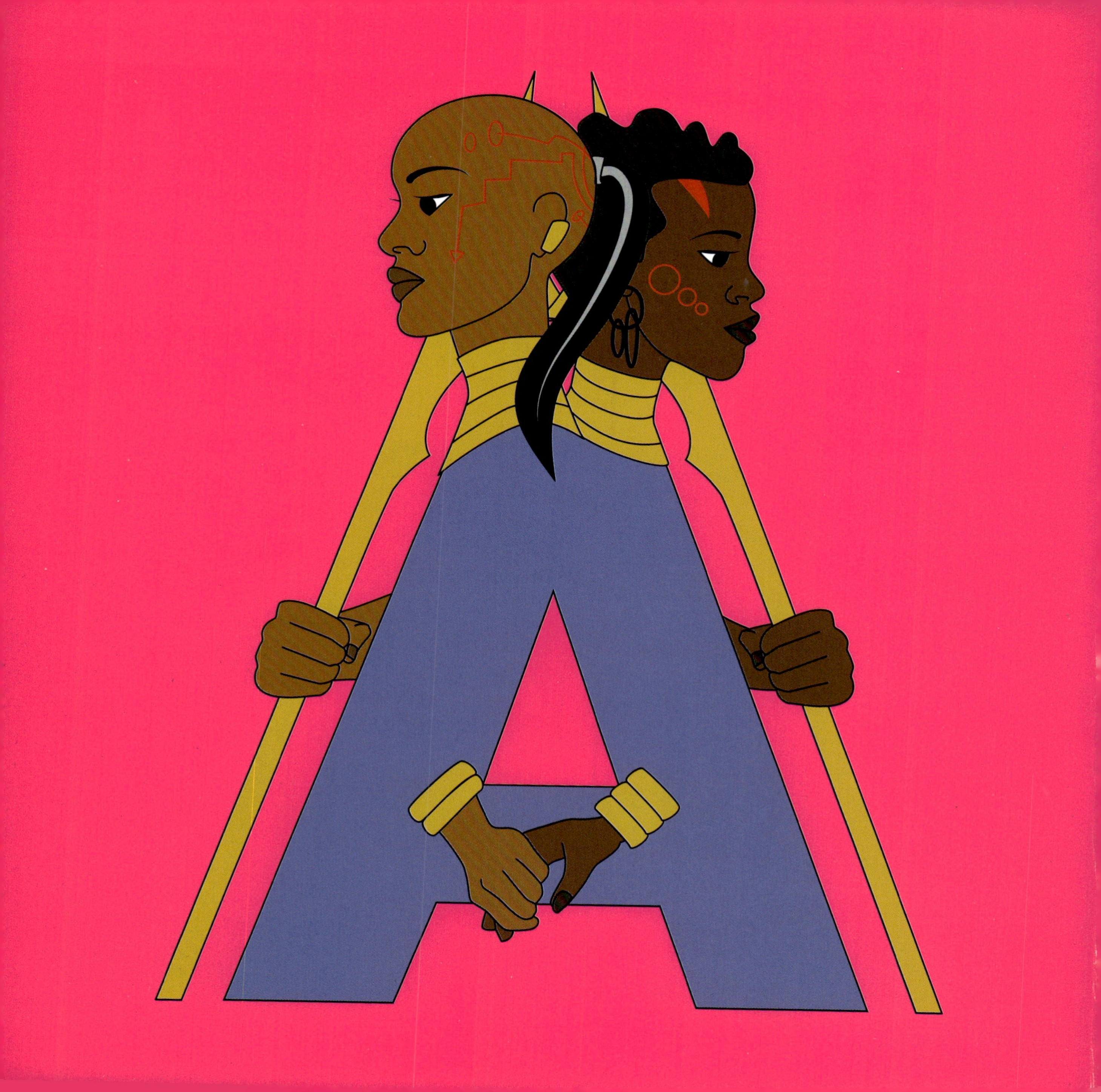

A is for **A**yo and **A**neka. As members of the Dora Milaje, these legendary Wakandan warriors proudly defended their nation alongside Black Panther. These days, they are known as the Midnight Angels, and their special armor helps them stand up for those in need.

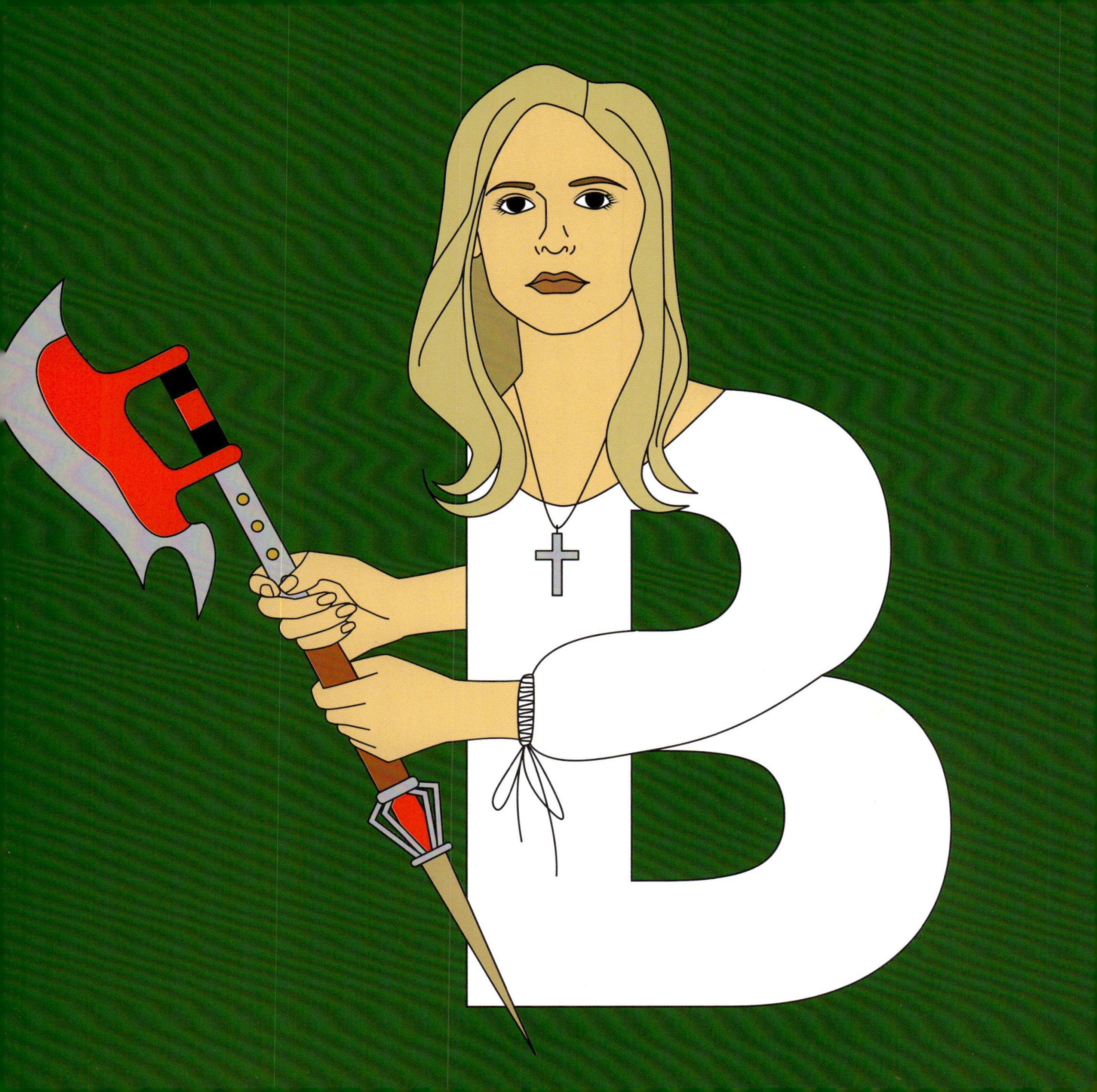
B

B is for **B**uffy Summers. Buffy is a Slayer and a member of the Scooby Gang. She protects the city of Sunnydale and the rest of the world from vampires, demons, and other evil creatures. As the Chosen One, Buffy wields wooden stakes and ancient scythes to fight dark forces!

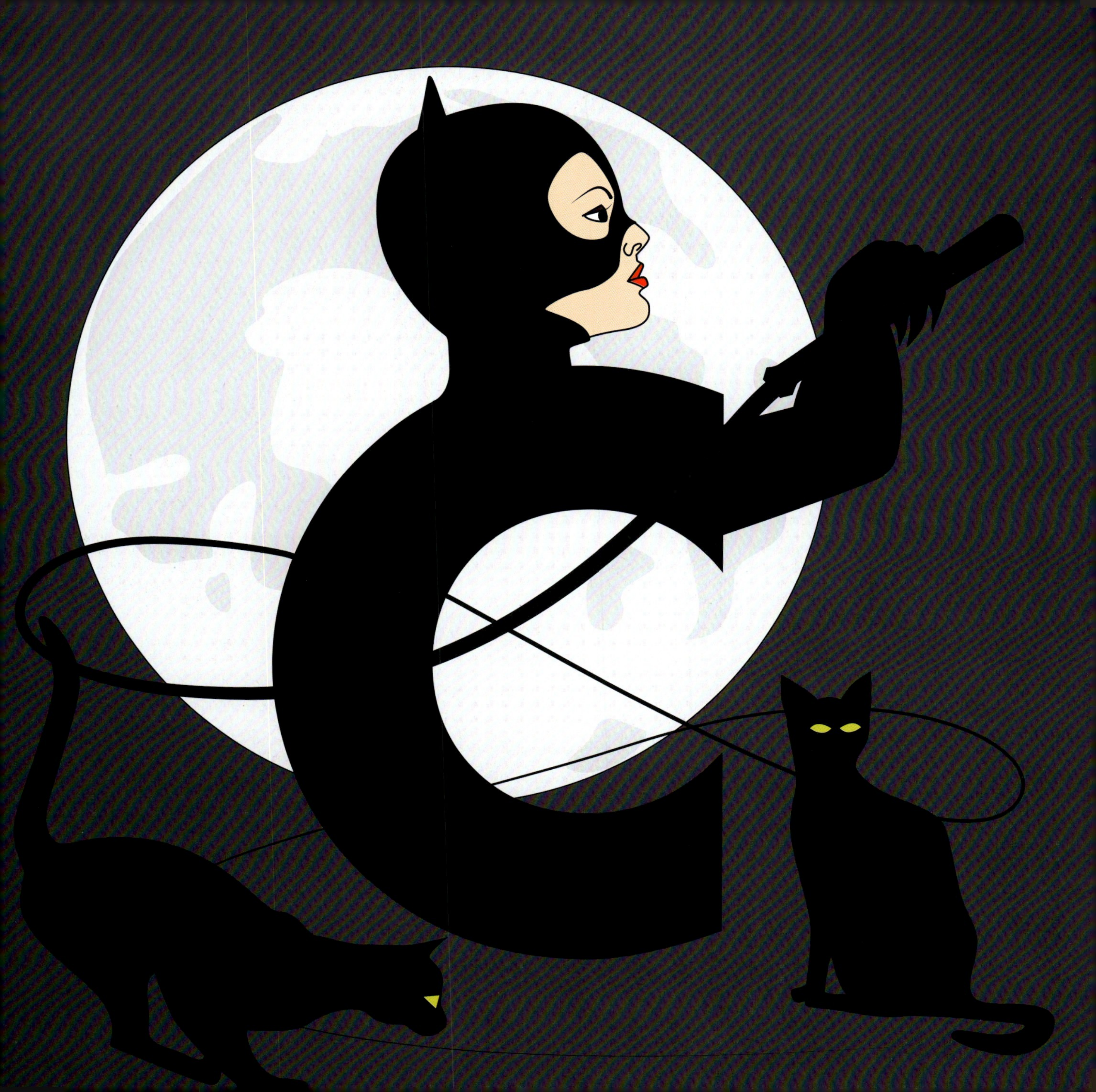

C is for Catwoman.
This Gotham cat burglar is always up for a bit of fun. Selina Kyle was originally one of Batman's most notorious nemeses. Her love for the Dark Knight changed her, and now she uses her acrobatic agility, martial arts talents, and signature whip for good.

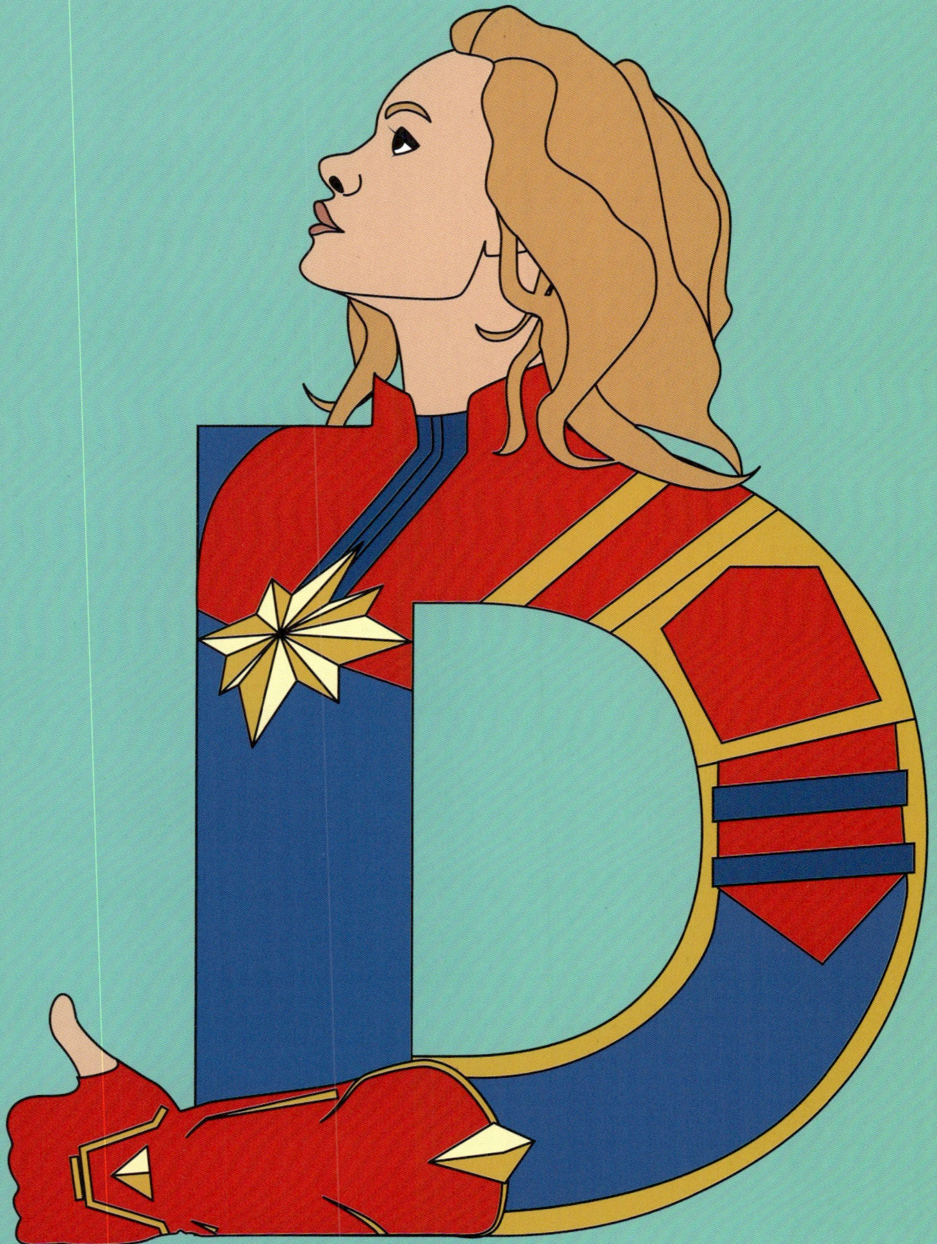

D is for Carol **D**anvers. Better known as Captain Marvel, this former Air Force pilot is half-Kree alien, half-human, and all legend. Her flying ability, super-strength, and energy-blasting powers help her protect the universe — sometimes alongside the mighty Avengers!

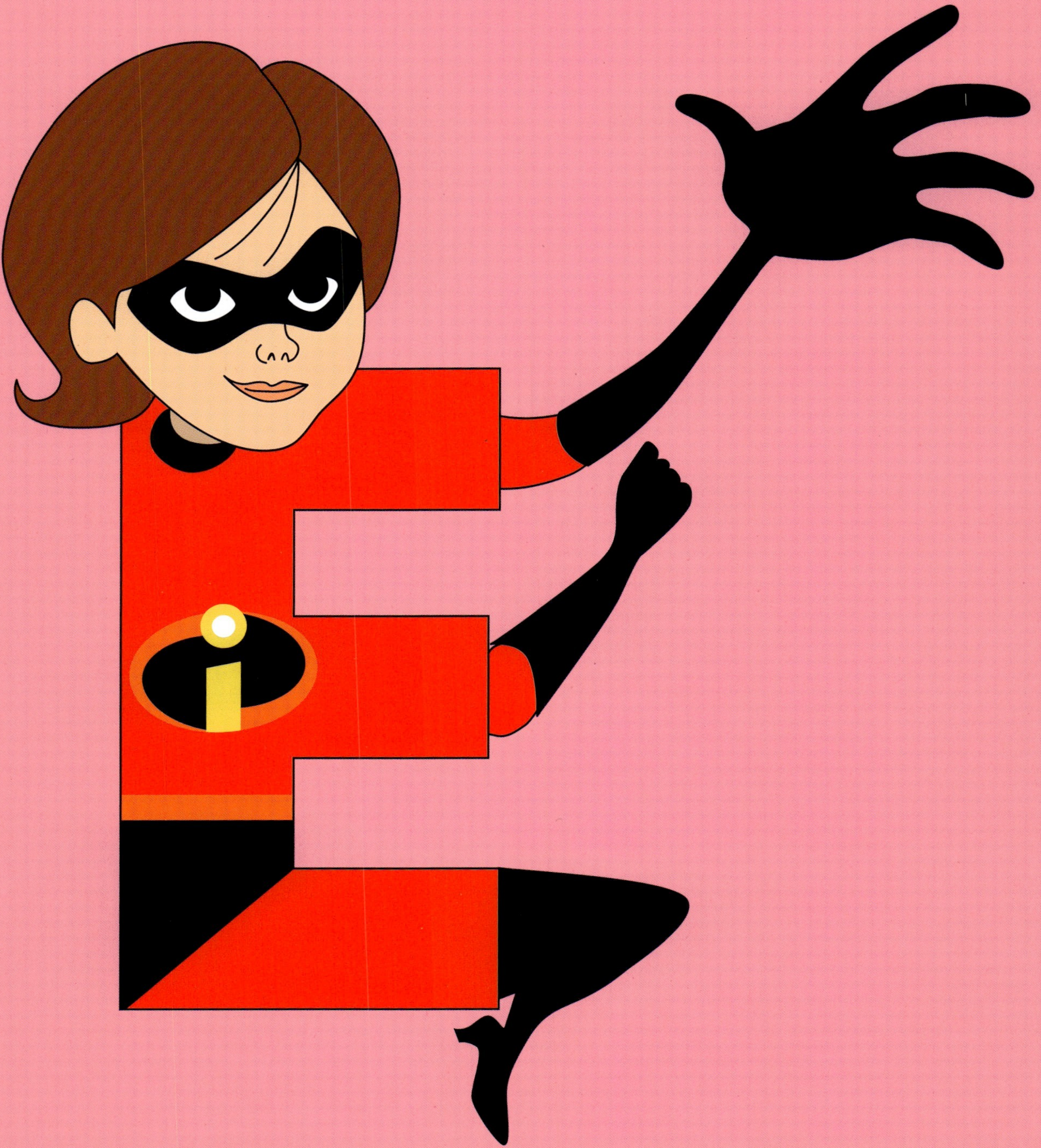

E is for **E**lastigirl.
Leave saving the world to men? Helen Parr doesn't think so! She might seem like a normal mom, but she's secretly Elastigirl of The Incredibles. By stretching her body into unbelievable shapes and sizes, she helps fight crime with her superpowered husband and kids.

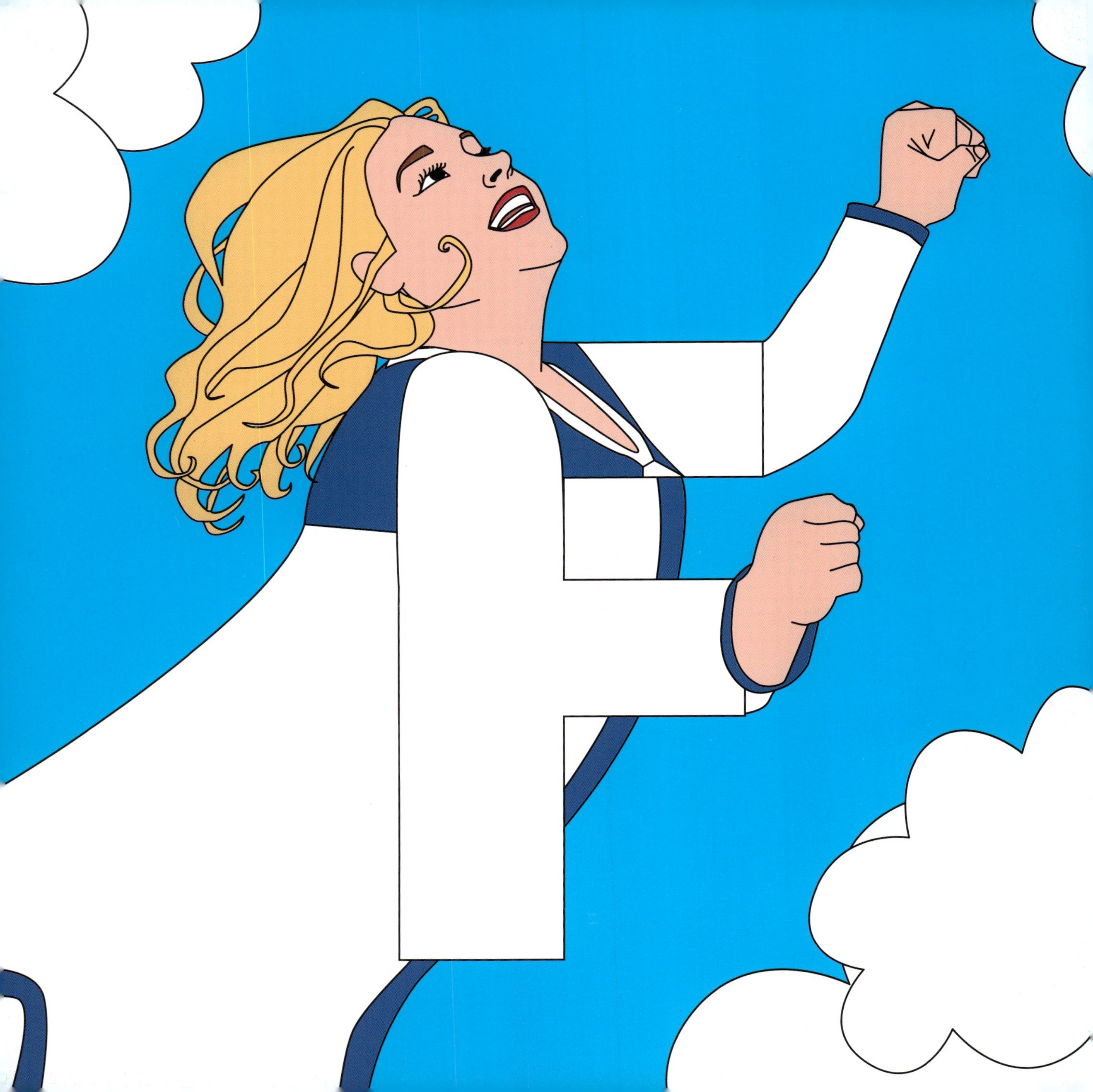

F is for **F**aith.
Faith Herbert was a massive science fiction fan growing up. Nowadays, this confident plus-sized hero has her own special set of Psiot powers: flight, telekinesis, and force field creation. Now known as Zephyr, Faith fights valiantly with her fellow Renegades.

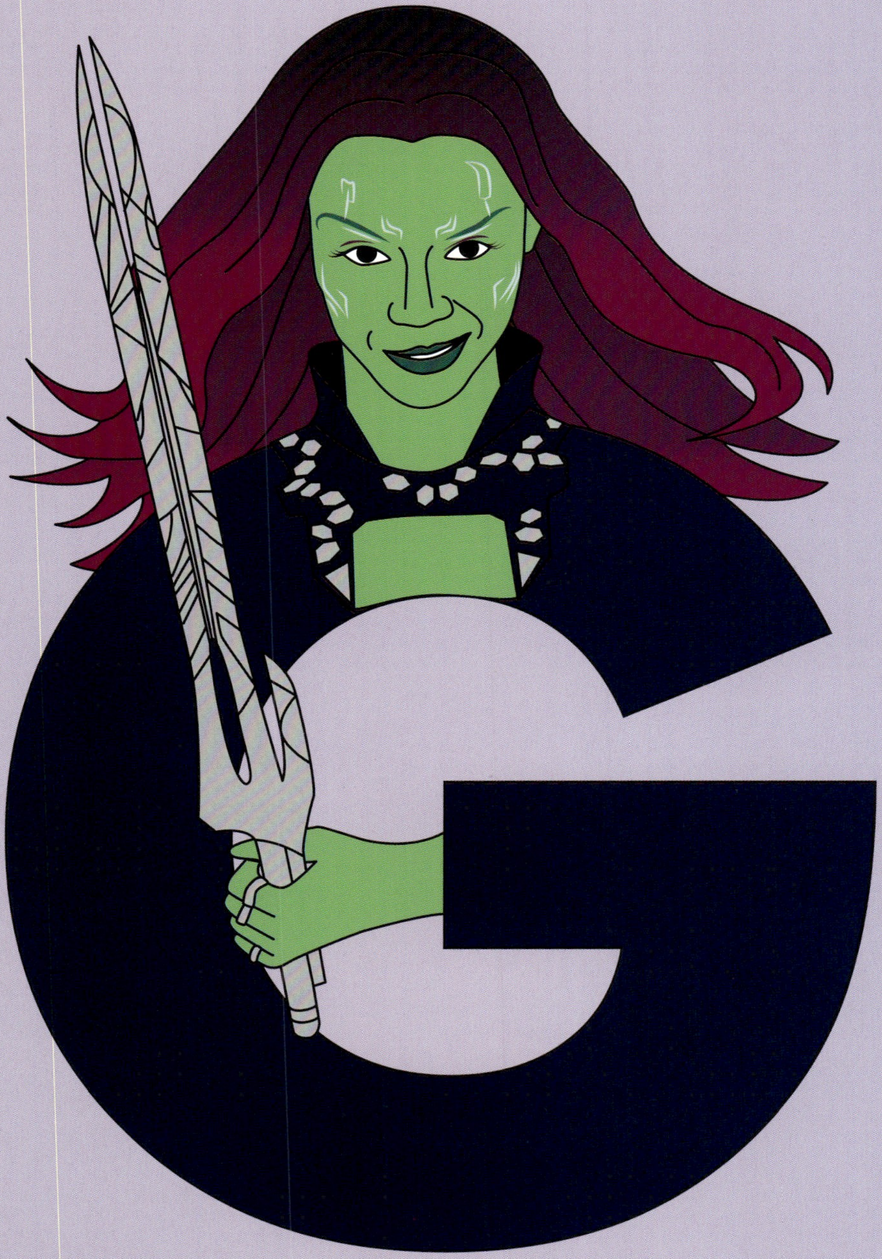
G

G is for **G**amora.
Whether using a sword, retractable knife, or her bare hands, Gamora is one of the most fearsome warriors in the universe. This green-skinned Guardian of the Galaxy was once a tool of destruction for Thanos, but she rebelled against the Mad Titan to fight for good.

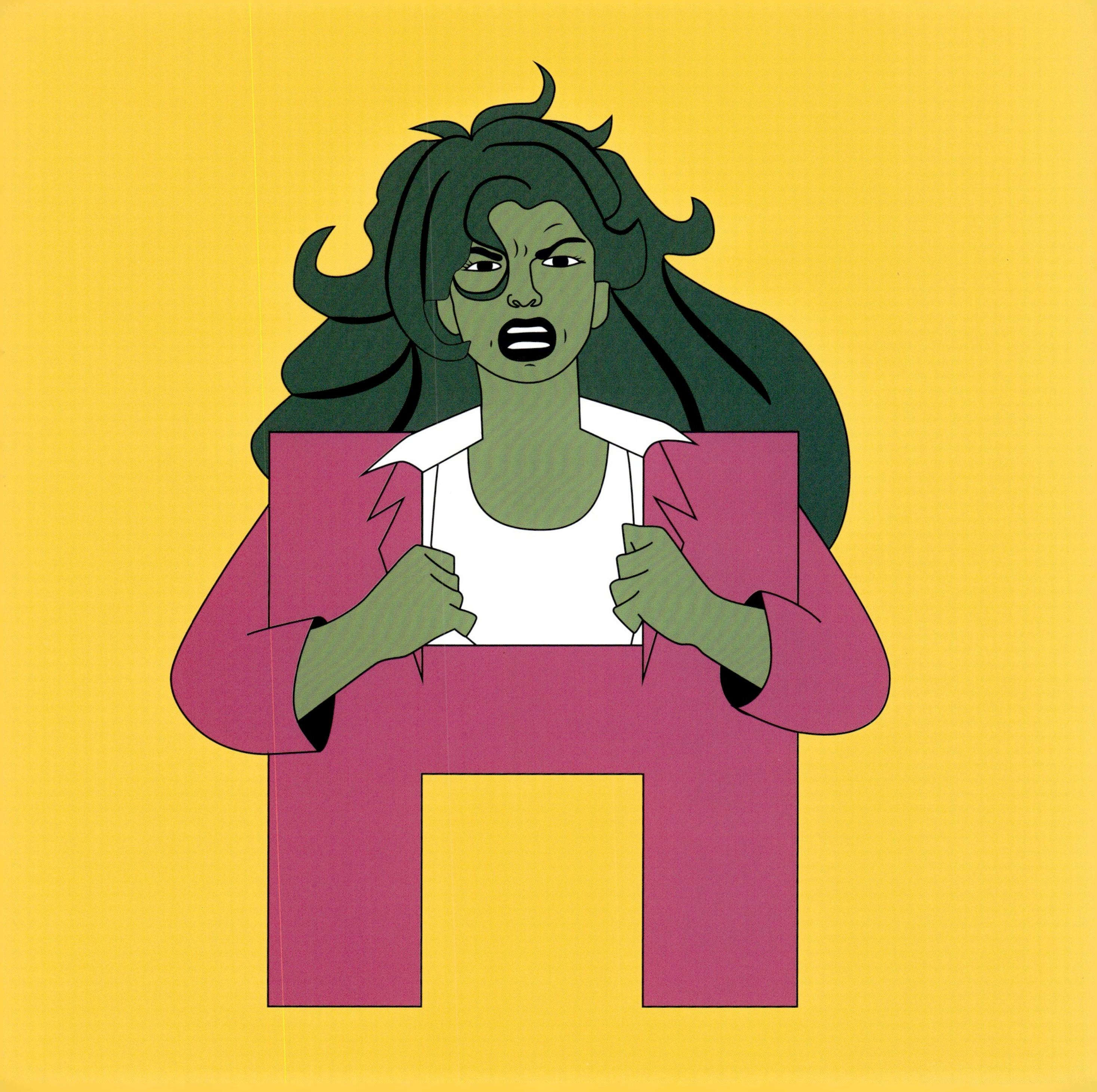

H is for She-**H**ulk. Jennifer Walters got her legendary powers after a blood transfusion from her cousin, Bruce Banner, who is known to most as the Incredible Hulk. Now this green, gamma-radiated superhero and lawyer fights evil inside and outside the courtroom.

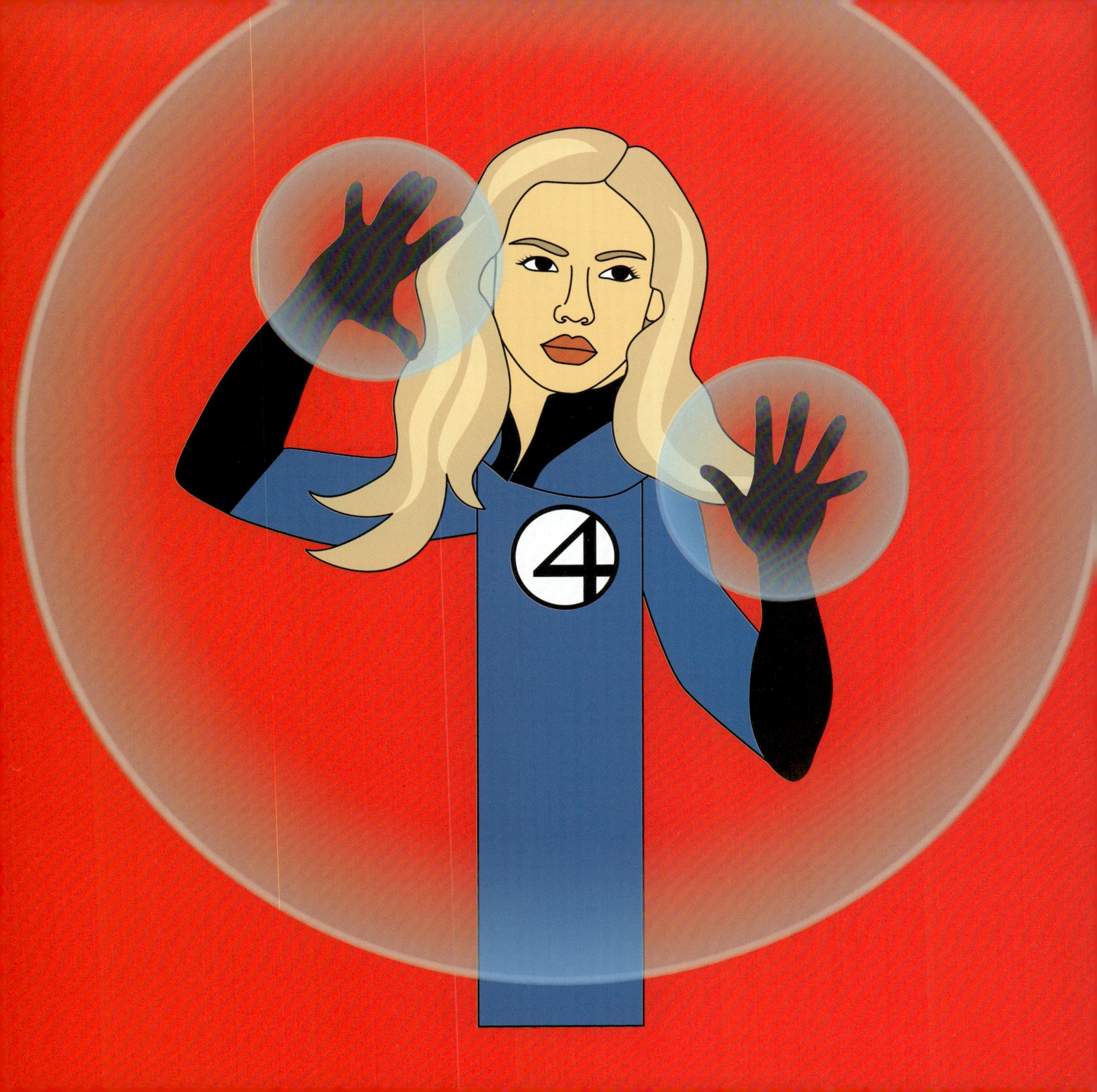

I is for **I**nvisible Woman.
This matriarch of the
Fantastic Four is an absolute
force. Susan Richards uses
her invisibility and force field
powers to battle alongside
her husband, Mr. Fantastic;
her brother, the Human Torch;
and one of her closest friends,
the Thing.

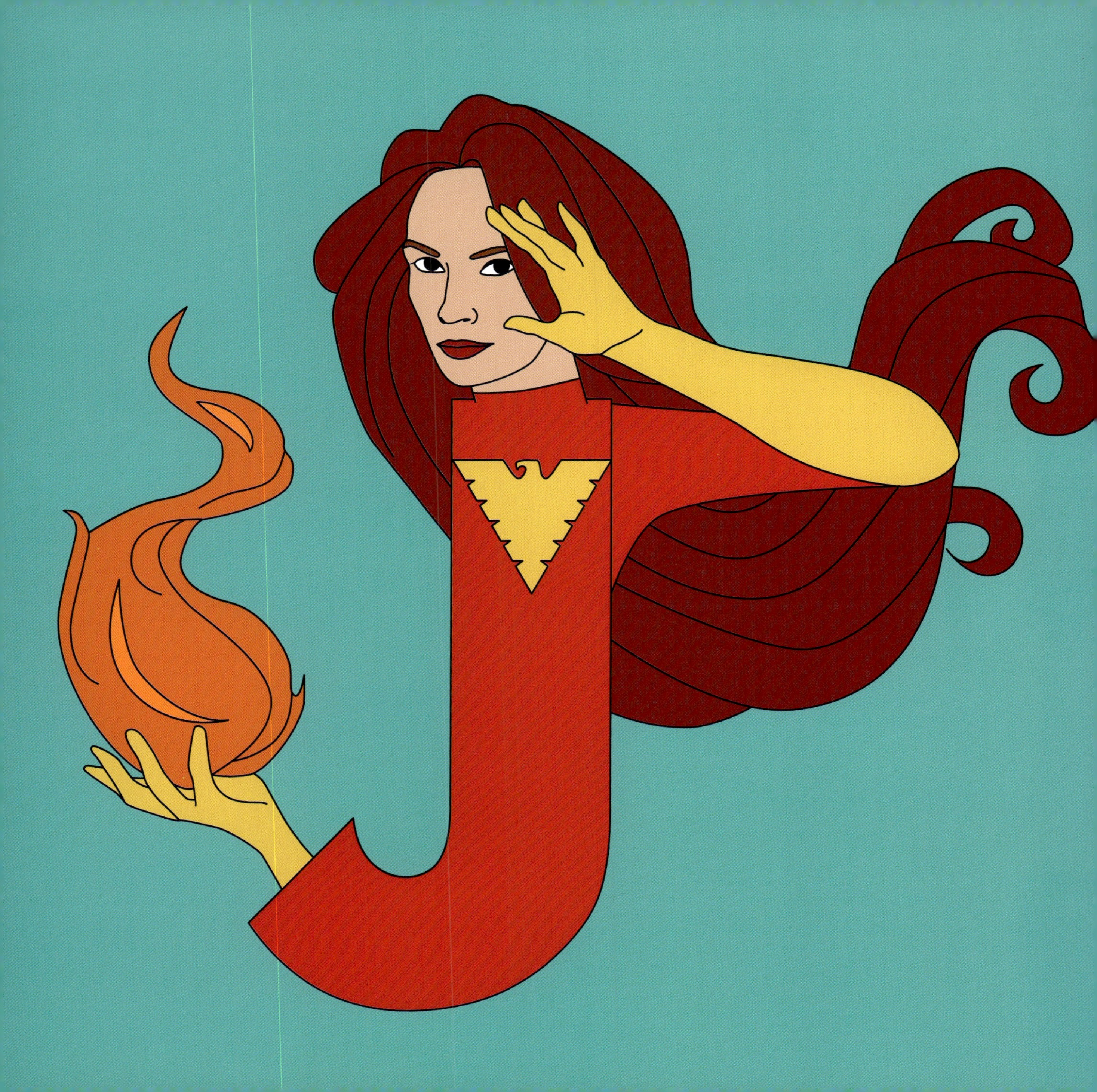

J is for **J**ean Grey.
A hero of many names,
Jean Grey made the ultimate
sacrifice when she destroyed
an out-of-control Phoenix
force within her. Lucky for
the love of her life, Cyclops,
Jean was brought back to
life and once again uses her
uncanny mental powers as
a member of the X-Men.

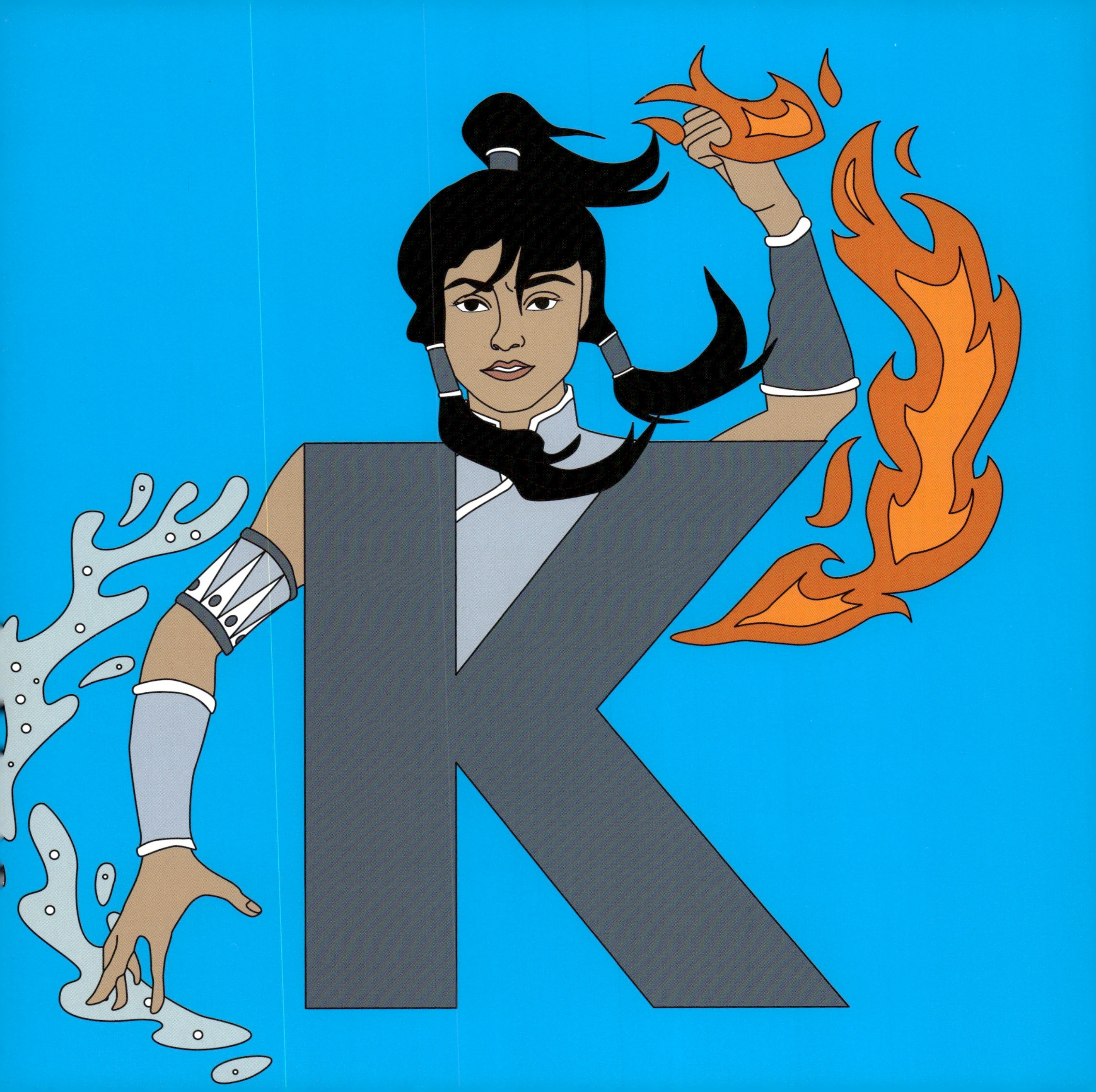
K

K is for Korra.
As a legendary Avatar and expert element bender, Korra brings balance to the spiritual and physical worlds. Her stubbornness gets her in trouble, but her determination and mastery of martial arts help her get out. Well ... that and her polar bear dog, Naga.

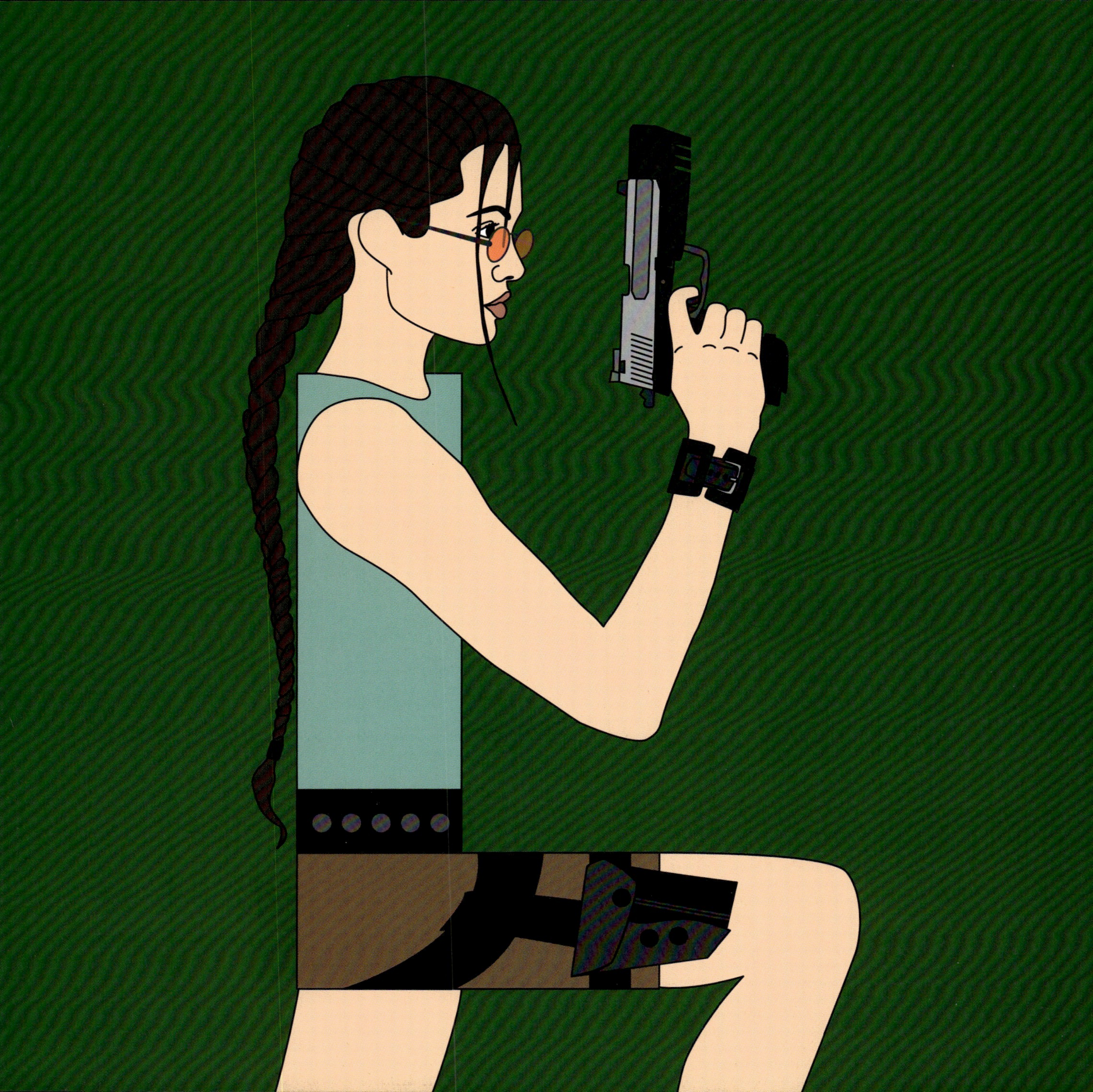

L is for Lara Croft.
You don't need superpowers to be a hero. This stealthy tomb raider uses her incredible intelligence, athleticism, and weaponry skills to search for ancient artifacts and treasures. She even unearths answers to some of life's greatest mysteries.

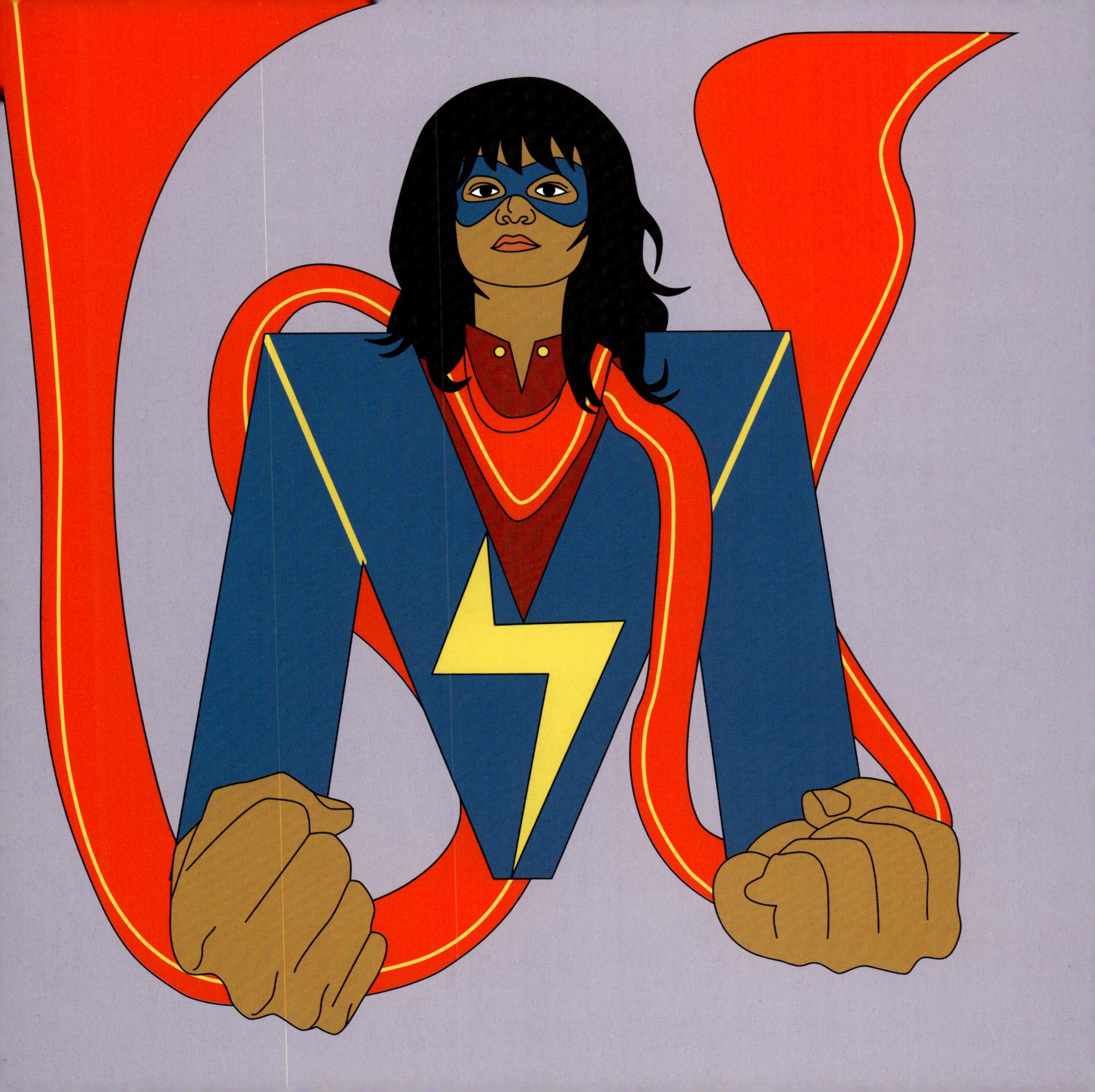

Mm

M is for Ms. **M**arvel.
Heroes come in all shapes,
sizes, and ages. As Ms. Marvel,
Pakistani-American Kamala
Khan uses her shapeshifting
and healing powers — and her
friend Bruno's tech wizardry —
to keep Jersey City safe.

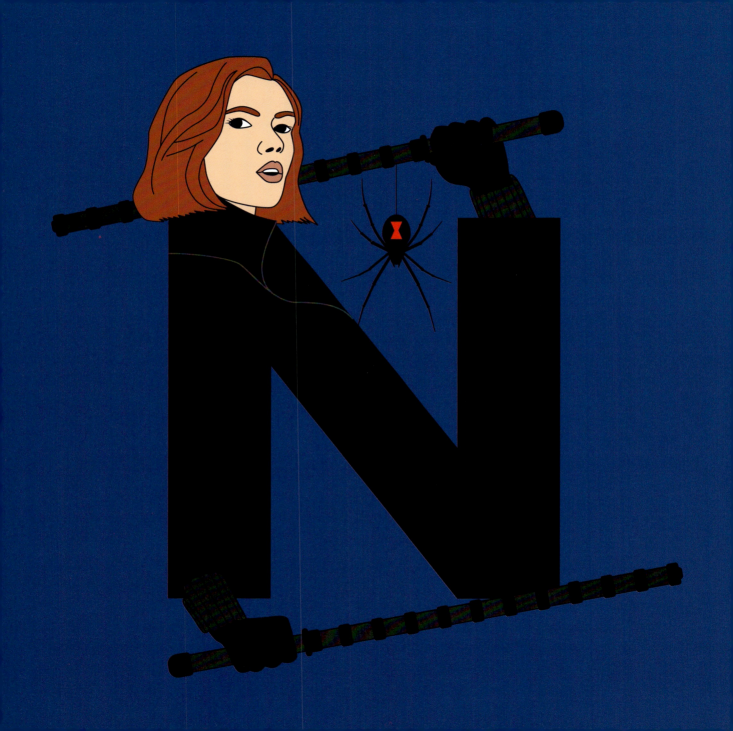

N is for **N**atasha Romanoff. This spy-turned-superhero relies on her secret Russian training and Widow's Bite electrical bracelets to atone for past sins. It doesn't matter whether she's working with the Avengers, Daredevil, or Wolverine — Black Widow always gets the job done.

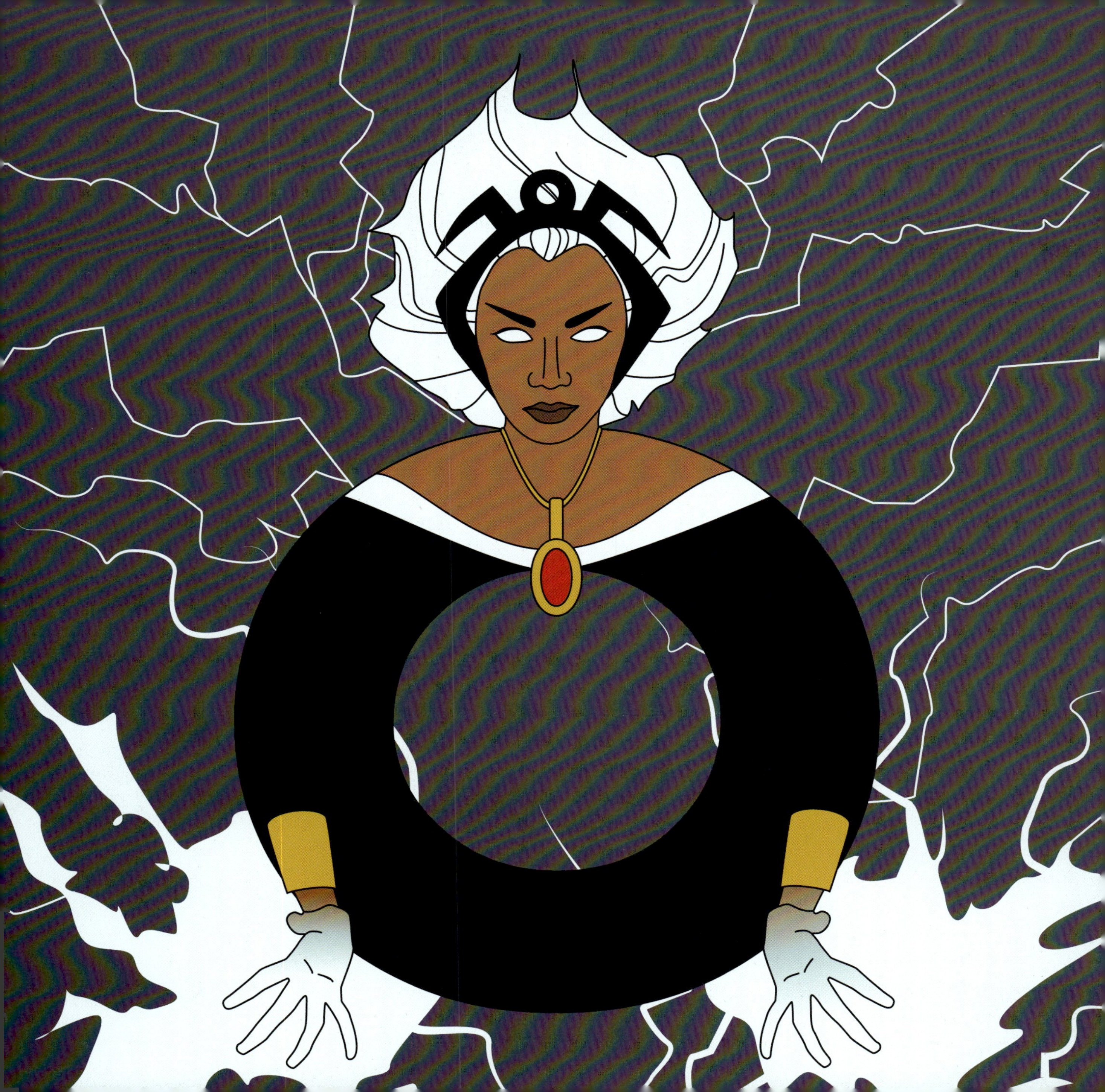

O is for Ororo Munroe. She transformed from a pickpocket on the streets of Egypt to one of the most powerful mutants on the planet. As Storm, her weather-controlling powers and uplifting leadership make her an indispensable member of the X-Men.

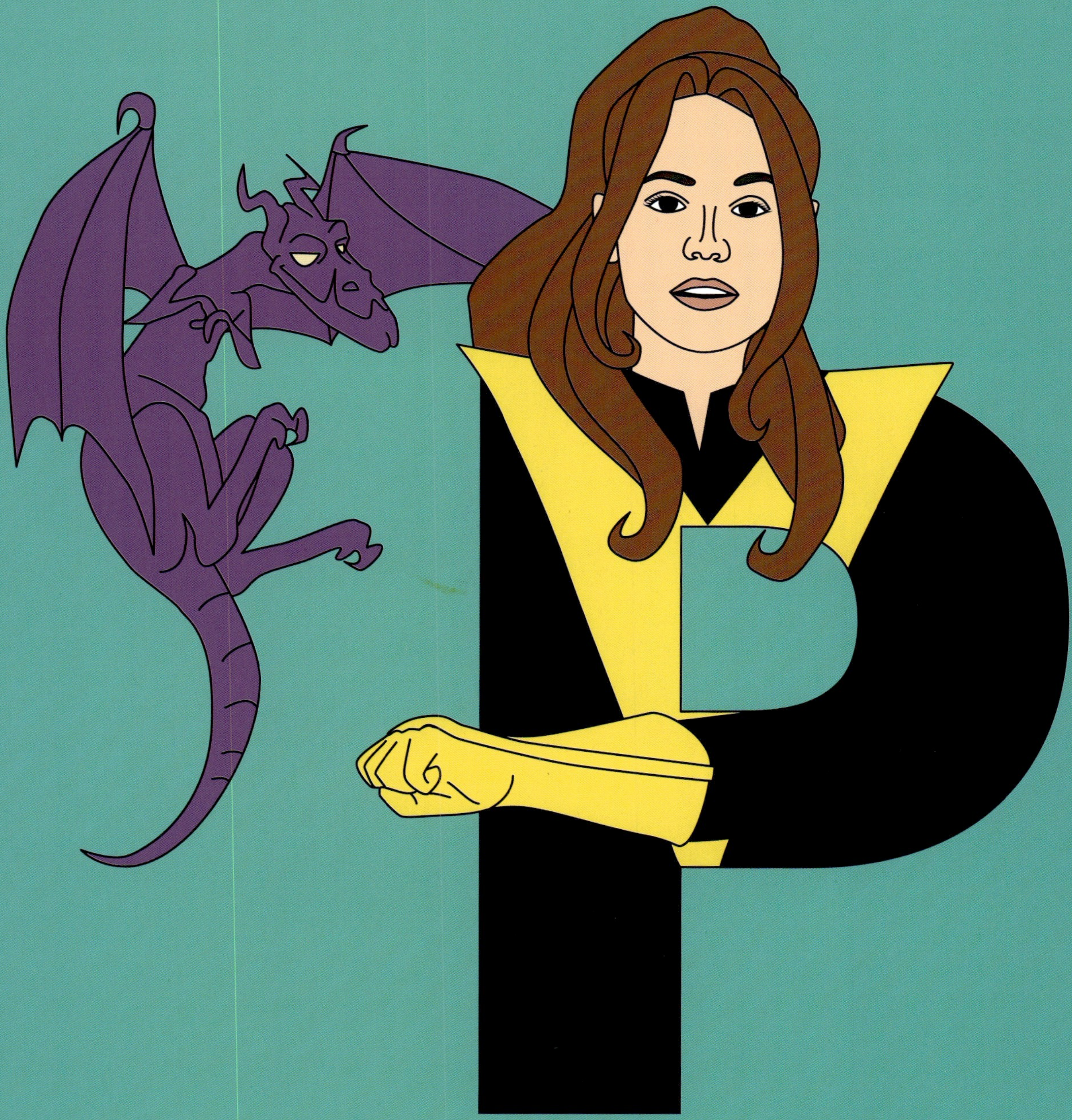

P is for Kitty Pryde.
Thanks to her superior
intelligence and phasing
powers, Kitty joined the
X-Men when she was only 13.
Since then, her mentor and
close friend, Storm, has
helped Shadowcat become
a dependable teammate.

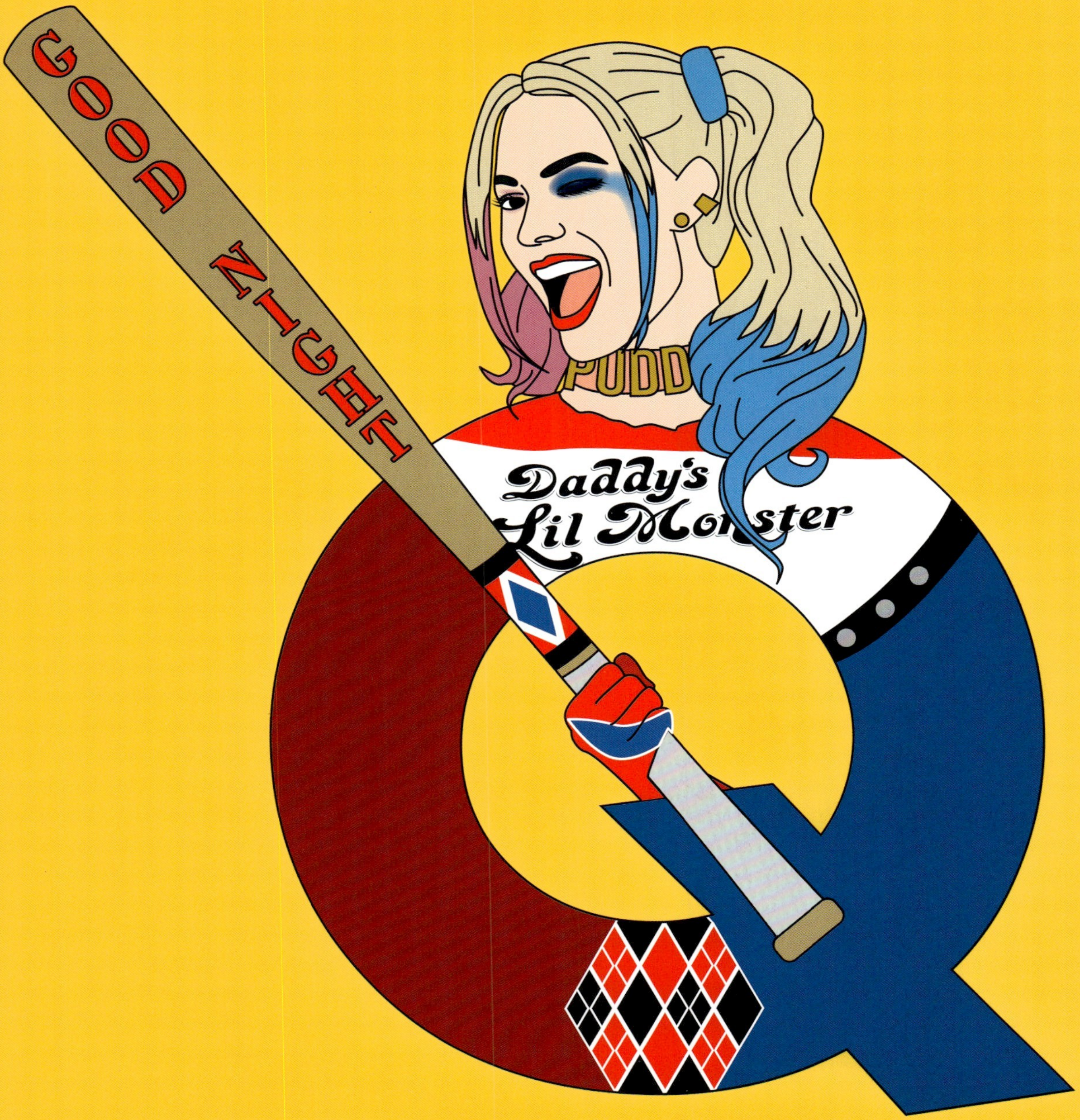
GOOD NIGHT
PUDD
Daddy's
Lil Monster

Q is for Harley **Q**uinn. Harley started out as a bad girl working alongside the Joker to defeat Batman. But after splitting from the Clown Prince of Crime, this former doctor now uses her legendary sense of humor and signature baseball bat for good.

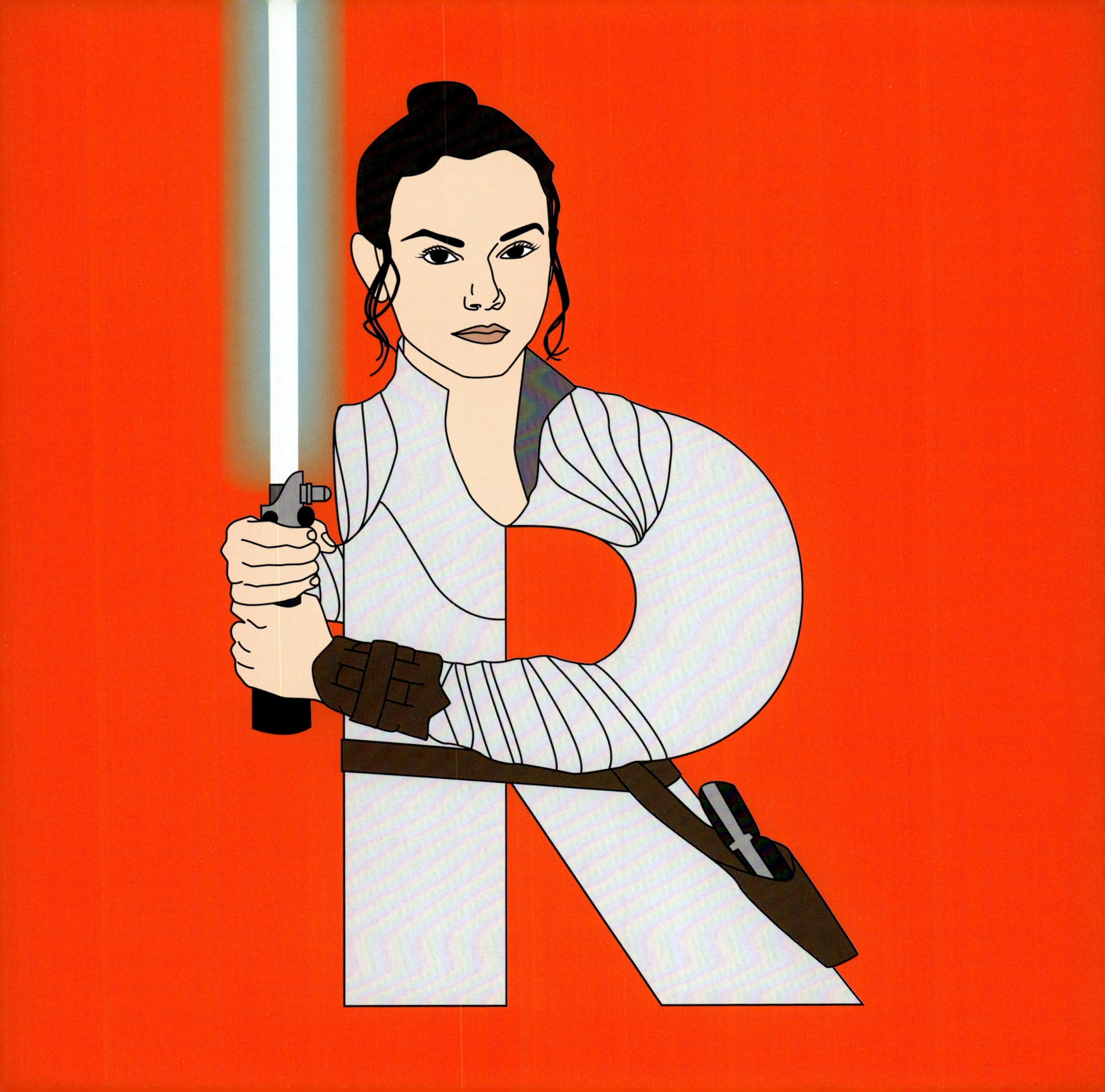

R is for **R**ey Skywalker. Rey's winding path took her all over the galaxy, from scavenging orphan to fearless Jedi Knight. She recently used the Force and her trusty blue lightsaber to defeat the evil First Order. Now, Rey's continued determination will help restore the Jedi Order.

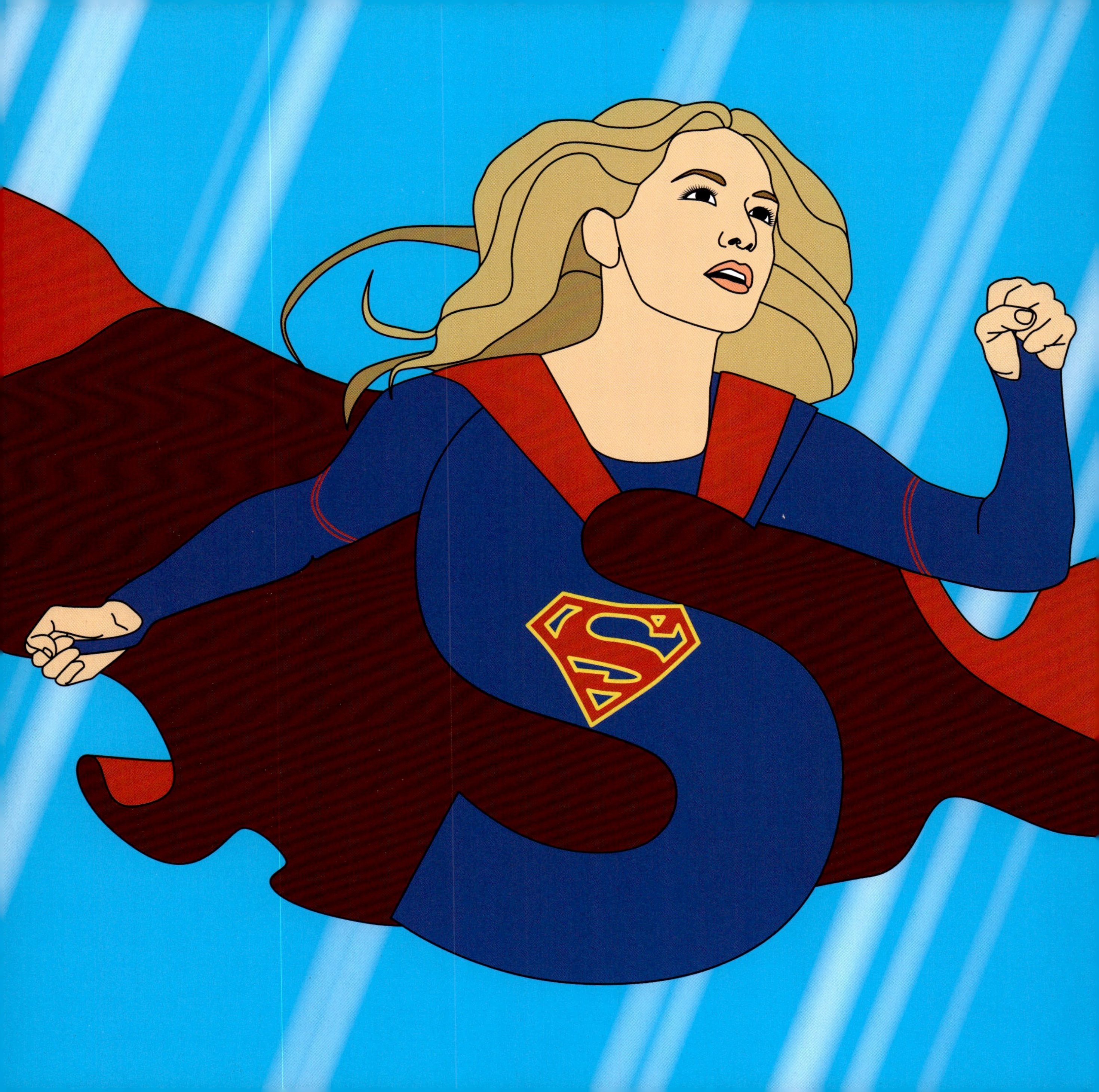

S is for **S**upergirl.
Move over, Superman — the Girl of Steel is here! Kara Zor-El traveled to Earth in a rocket from the planet Krypton. Using her incredible speed, strength, and flight powers, this legendary teen fights through her own mistakes to topple the bad guys.

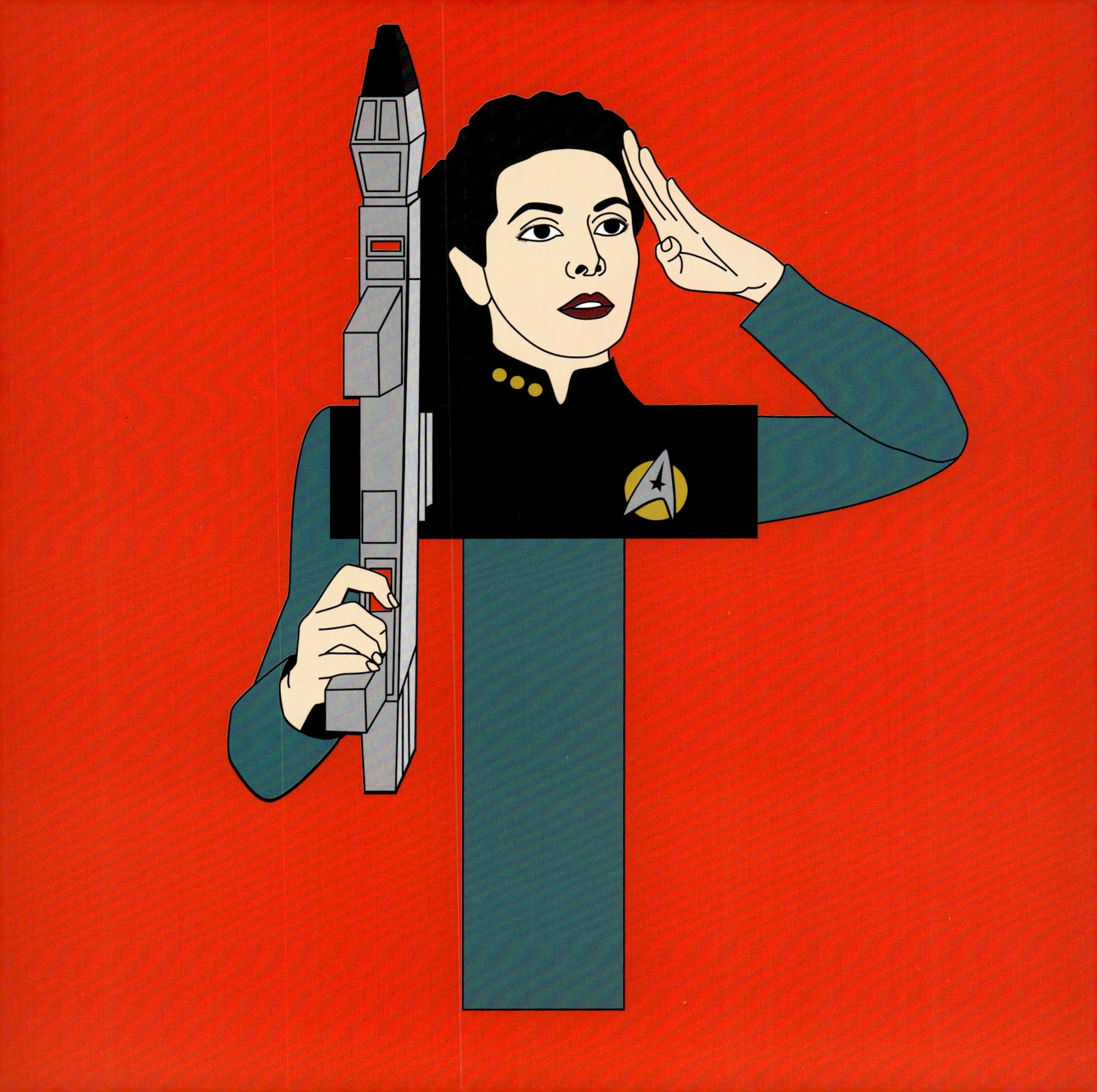

Tt

T is for Deanna **T**roi. With her ability to sense emotions, this half-human, half-Betazoid (and full-on chocolate lover) helps her fellow Starfleet officers through some of their most difficult times during their Star Trek. She's a counselor by title, but a hero by deed.

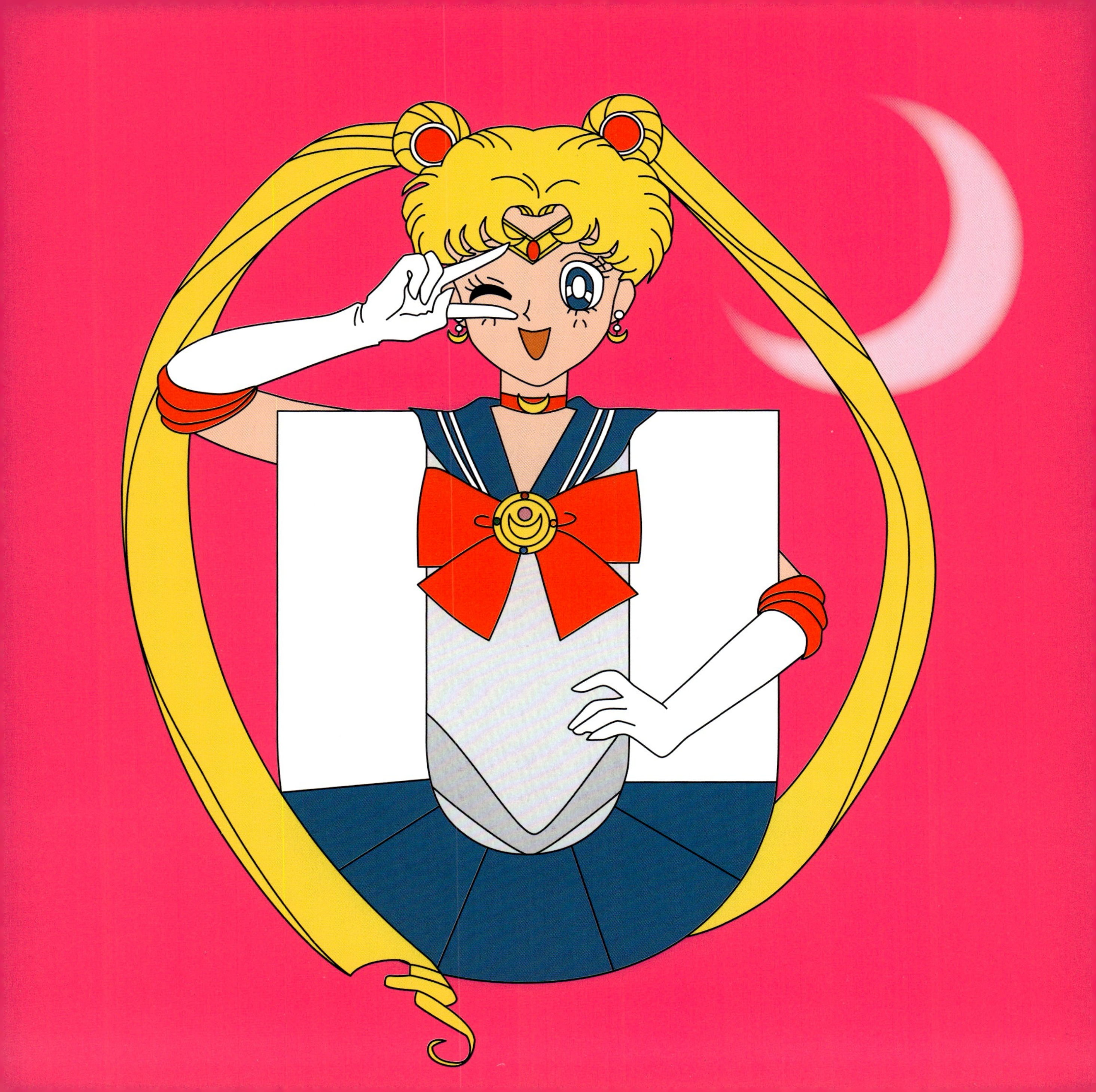

U is for Usagi Tsukino.
In the name of the moon,
she will punish all bad guys!
As the heroic Sailor Moon —
the Sailor guardian of love
and justice — Usagi fights
alongside her fellow Sailor
Soldiers to keep the immensely
powerful Silver Crystal out of
the wrong hands.

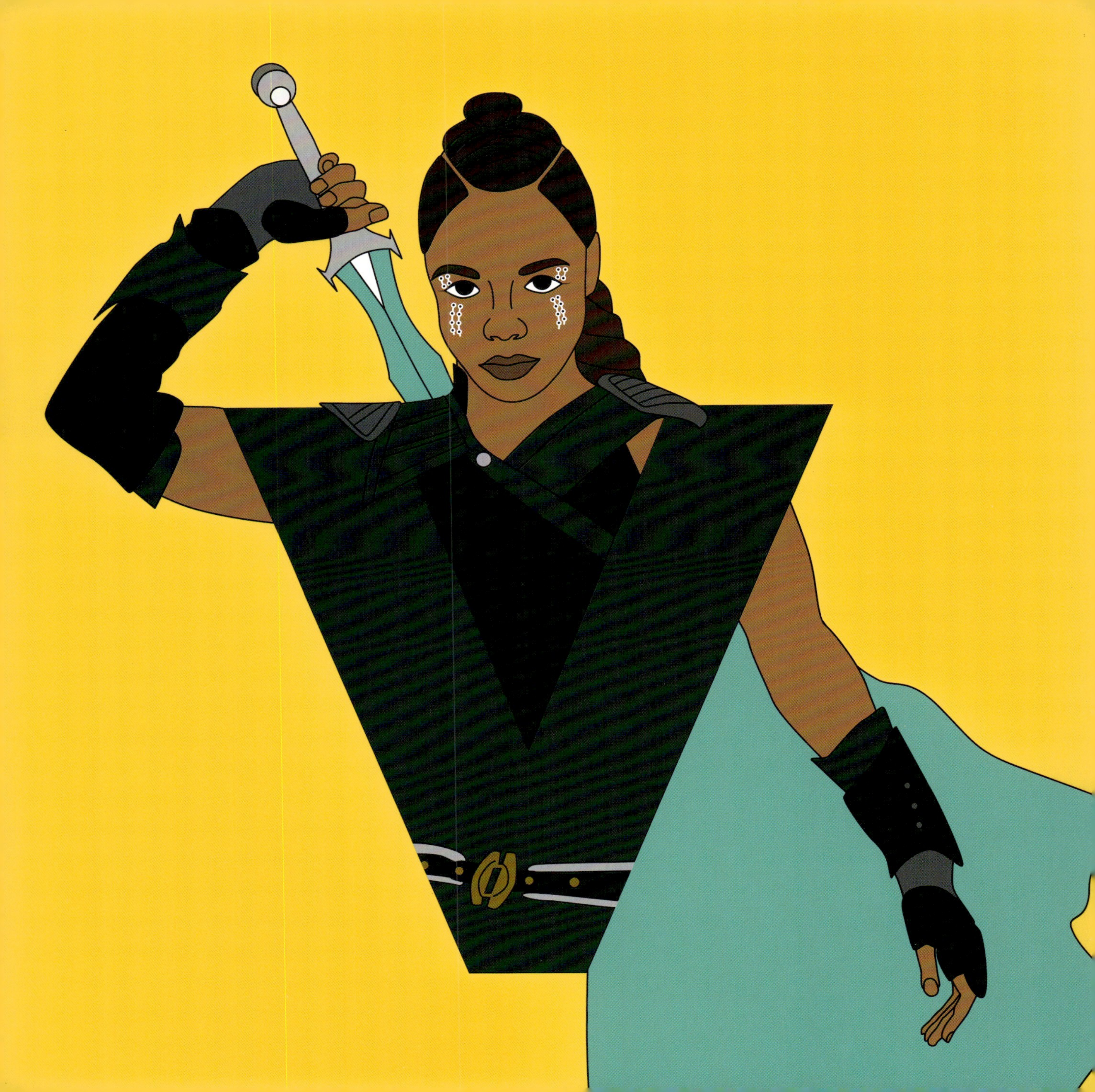

V is for **V**alkyrie.
This legend never backs down from a fight. The last of a breed of Asgardian warriors, Valkyrie possesses super strength, stamina, speed, and sword handling skills. She's deadly with her Dragonfang blade in hand, and she's an expert pilot, too.

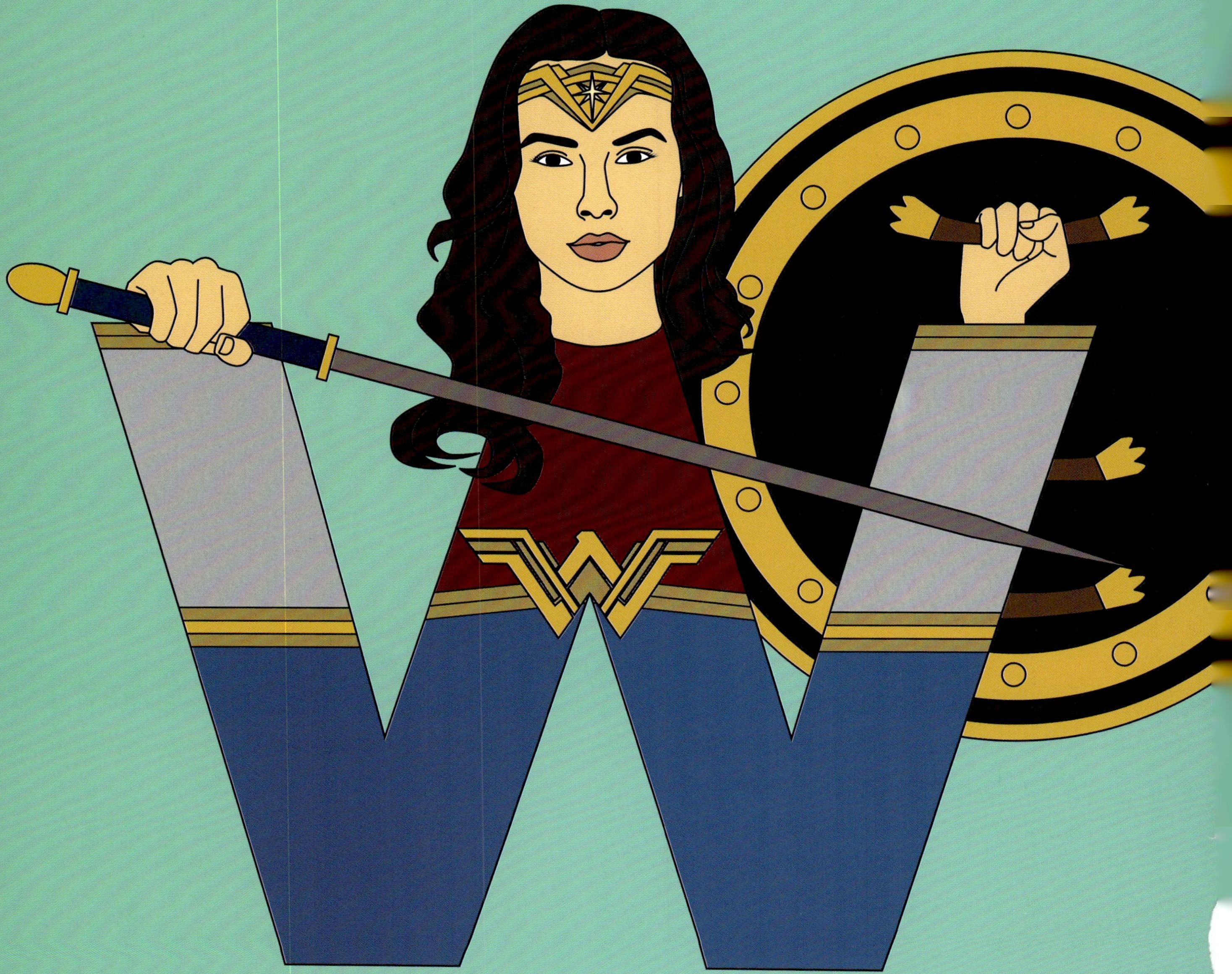

W is for **W**onder Woman. A proud Amazonian warrior princess, Diana's super strength and flight ability make her invaluable to the Justice League. But her bulletproof bracelets, invisible jet, and Lasso of Truth make her truly legendary.

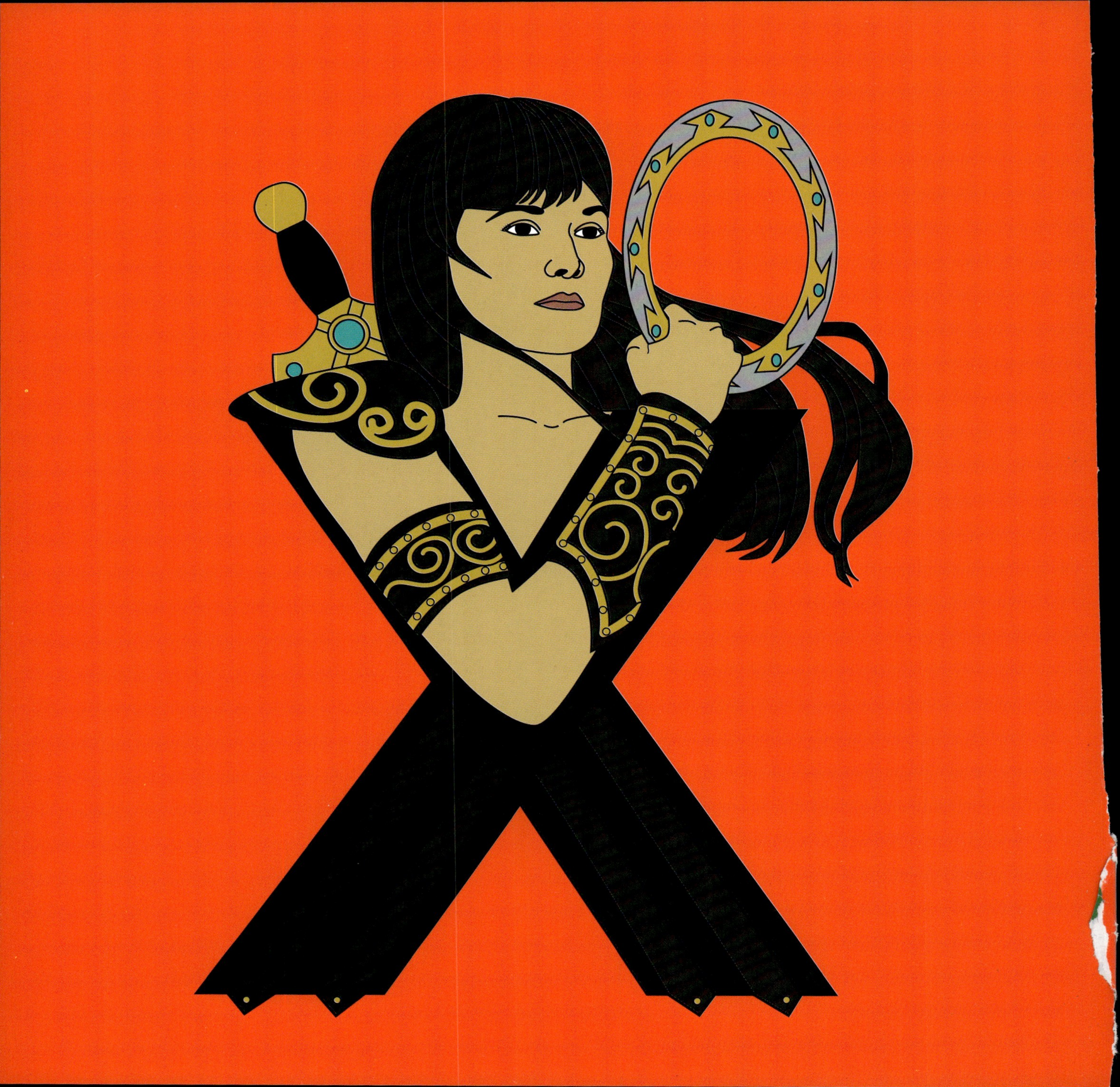

X is for **X**ena.
This Warrior Princess expertly wields her sword and Chakram to make amends for her dark past as the Destroyer of Nations. With help and inspiration from friends Hercules and Gabrielle, Xena travels the long, hard road to redemption.

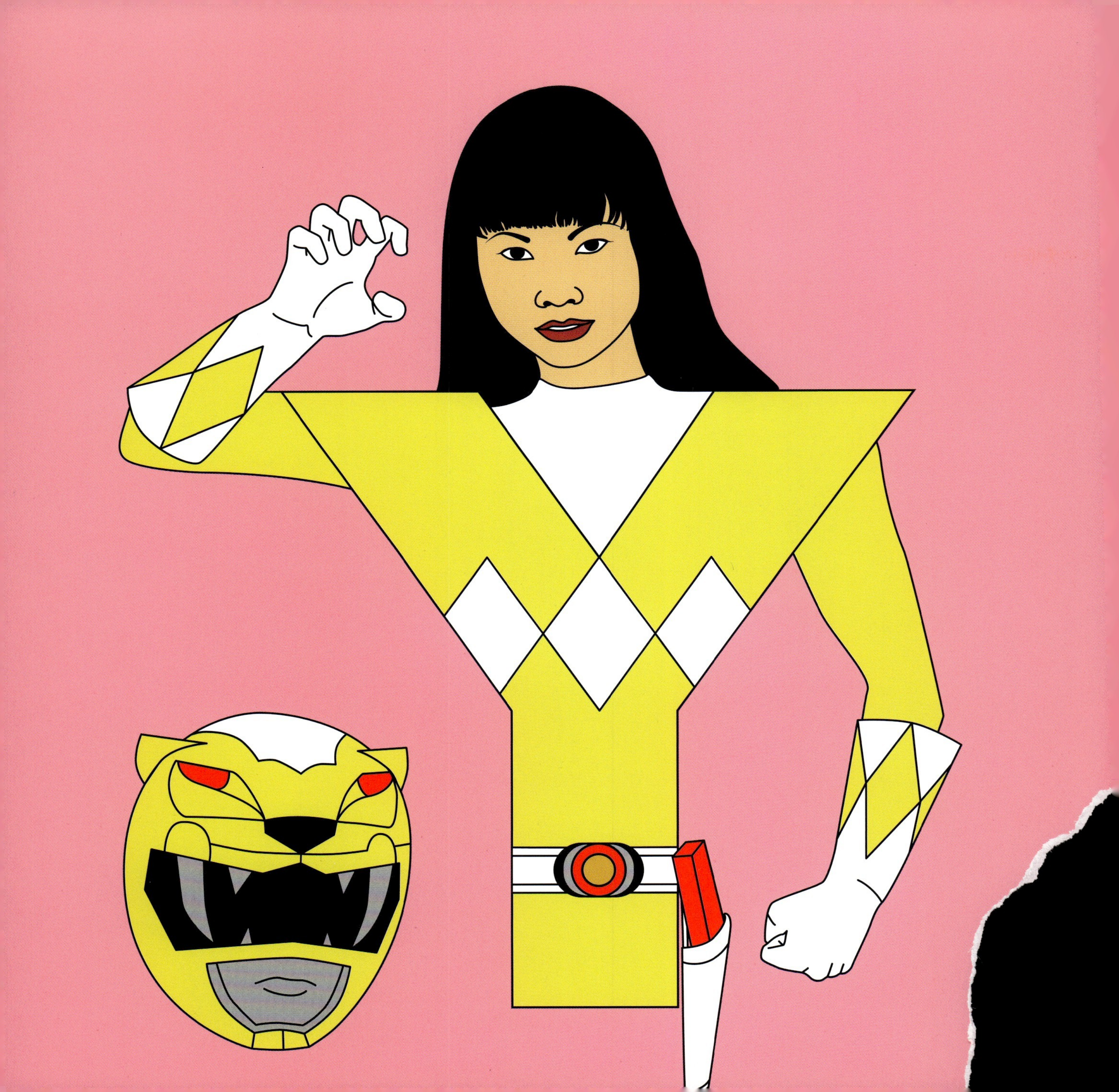

Y is for **Y**ellow Ranger Trini Kwan. This Mighty Morphin Power Ranger uses her martial arts skills and Sabertooth Tiger Dinozord to take on Rita Repulsa and her evil Putty Patrol. With a cool head and math and science know-how, it's no wonder she's a legendary earth-saving hero.

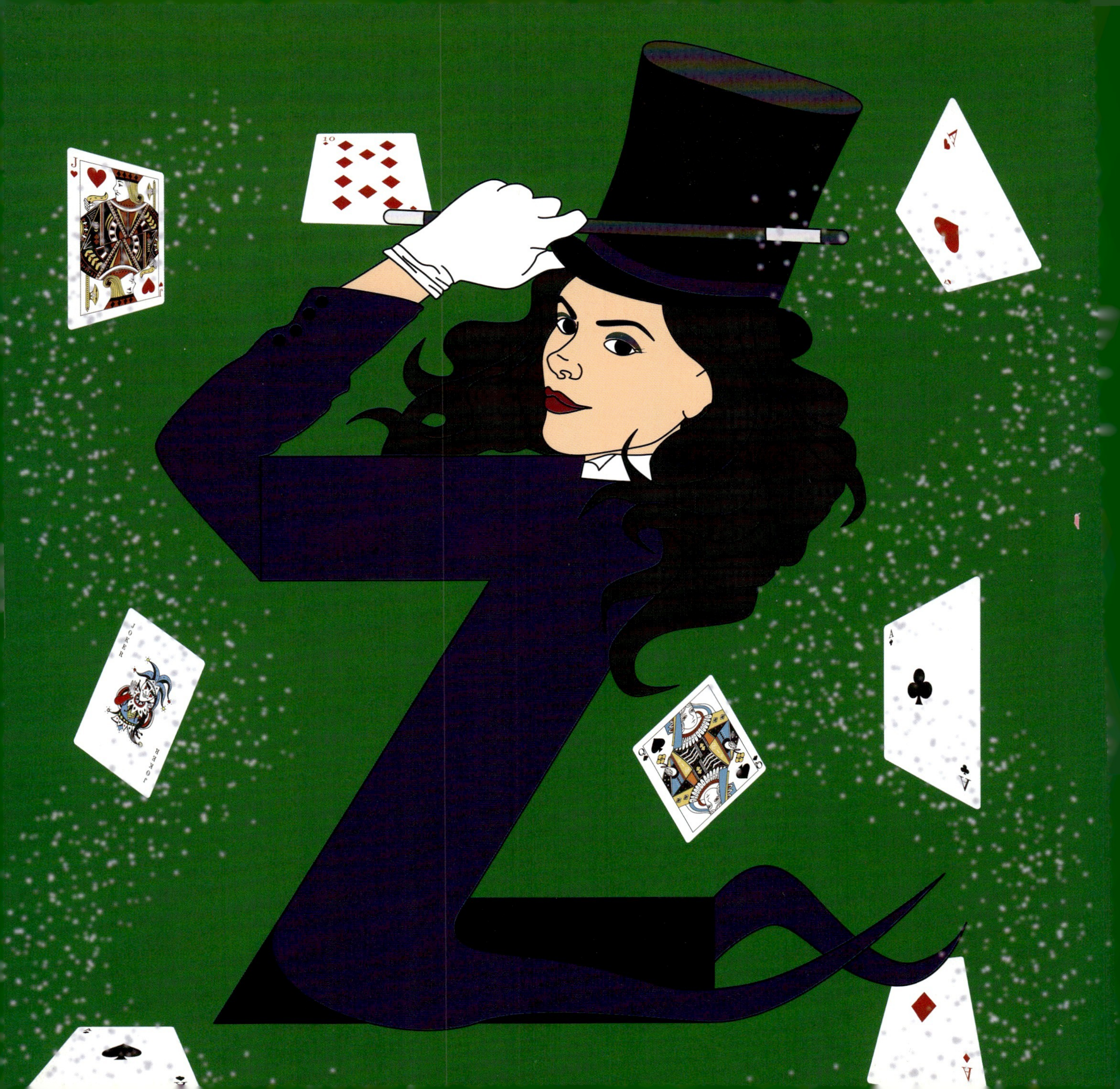
JOKER

Z is for **Z**atanna.
Step right up and watch this legendary magician as she manipulates reality to save the day yet again! This occasional Justice Leaguer casts spells backward, and her incredible imagination helps her escape tight jams and assist those in need.

The ever-expanding legendary library

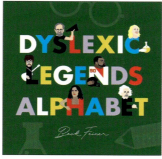

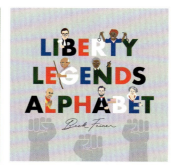

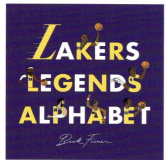

EXPLORE THESE LEGENDARY ALPHABETS & MORE AT WWW.ALPHABETLEGENDS.COM

SUPERHERO LEGENDS ALPHABET - WOMEN
www.alphabetlegends.com

Published by Alphabet Legends Pty Ltd in 2021
Created by Beck Feiner
Copyright © Alphabet Legends Pty Ltd 2021

9780645200119

Printed and bound in China.